On Narrowness

Also by Claire Crowther

Stretch of Closures
The Clockwork Gift

Claire Crowther

On Narrowness

Shearsman Books

First published in the United Kingdom in 2015 by
Shearsman Books
50 Westons Hill Drive
Emersons Green
BRISTOL
BS16 7DF

Shearsman Books Ltd Registered Office
30–31 St. James Place, Mangotsfield, Bristol BS16 9JB
(this address not for correspondence)

www.shearsman.com

ISBN 978-1-84861-390-4

ACKNOWLEDGEMENTS
Thanks are due to the editors of the following publications where
many of the poems, or early versions of them, first appeared:
Journals: *Art World, Blackbox Manifold, Iota, Long Poem Magazine,
Magma, Molly Bloom, New Statesman, New Walk, Poem, Poetry and
Audience, PN Review, Poetry Review, Poetry Salzburg Review, Poetry Wales,
Qualm, The Reader, Shearsman, Tears in the Fence*

Anthologies: 'Trompe L'oeil' appeared in *The Best British Poetry 2013* (Salt
2013), 'Lullaby' appeared in *Lyric Beats* (Rhythm 'n Muse 2013). 'Gold
Moment' appeared in *Drifting Down the Lane* (Moon and Mountain
2013), 'Self-Portrait as Windscreen', 'The Alices' and 'Heritage'
appeared in *Maps and Legends* (Nine Arches Press 2013).
'Victorian Harvest' was commissioned for *Magma*'s Short Poem
Competition award ceremony 2013.

for Keith

Contents

The Alices

I said he was brillig and I meant it.
He stood in the hall of a friend's house
offering extra as simply as a hostess
carrying crockery, the only one of us

who has actually fought the jabberwock,
whose face we see on News at Ten,
whose name is called at tribunals, who defies
James Naughtie on Today. He talked

about mome raths, saying hesitantly,
'If the raths don't outgrabe.'
I loathed seeing him like that, stooping
below somebody's lintel, being slithy.

'It's not about gyring,' he snapped.
But it was. Later he told me how
after a tough meeting, in the distance
he'd seen me climbing out of a car,

my flesh suggesting something else to save.
The houses our set restored fetch fortunes.
Is that better behaviour? A brillig affair!
So special a person to have taken to wabe.

I thought, they all do it, the toves.
The tension, the criticism they get
for neglecting their children, the fear
of borogoves. We support them,

us Alices. But we're mome. 'To me
you could never be mome,' he said
'whatever you decide,' as he left.

Captured Women

And in that house there was a room
That was hung with many drawings
Of women with their mouths tight
Shut, lips making a point:
'Why do you stand in front of us?
Why stand there? Why not go?'

One dipped her curls forward
Thoughtfully: 'Why don't you hang?
When will you go?' Their hair, serious
Expansion of each, upwards, sideways,
A boundary against the questions:
'Why are we on the brink of you?'

The pencil asked what hair weighs
And drew it to cover the tucked-away
Technology of ear. Listen.
The captured women ask: 'Why
Do we hang in front of you?
Why hang here? Why don't we go?'

The jib of them, their hissing sound
Like woodpeckers or worried finches
Considering a swing at the seeds
Before flight from the sparrowhawk:
'Why do we hang here while you stand?
Why don't we go? Why don't we go?'

Coincidence of Bodies

for Beatrice Tinsley, astronomer, 1941-81

The heavier I was, the more I shaped space
round me. Mass curves space. Come on eclipses, you never
could have blocked me. I curved new space.

But my own flesh was moon. It eclipsed
the larger body of sun in the coincidence of distance
that makes them equal, that allows

measurement of the bend of stars.
I was flesh. Had I been only that mass coordinating
old allegories that must be Love

or Sensuality, I would have appealed
for the fleshlessness I have now, I'd have begged not to be
a monument of blood.

And if I'd survived till fallen flesh
changed my shape so it wasn't hunted or held up, would I
have resolved the paradox of flesh –

that I was made of more than I am?
Mars, you wore only a helmet half off to show us flesh
is too frail for battle. My fabric now

is lighter than flesh, the blue of galaxies.
I am what has been proved of the coincidence of bodies,
given I'm not shortlived and can eclipse.

Emotion at Work, 1970

The workers in Mental Health walked out
behind their leader. Our new team
presented the family as one
big unhappy world of disciplines:
geography, classics, psychology.
That year, I was literature.

Outside our meeting, a manhole,
cover removed; a fall like that hurts
groin and hip. A weak floor
gave way. My foot dangled into
the room below. I fell running
from a police dog once. My heart-

shaped zip pulls dangled from
Suelia's ankles: my desert boots.
Under her bed, piles of files.
That was wrong. Being single,
I took the small room and painted
the walls red, red, red and yellow.

I left the office to section Joe
the Axe, left Charlotte murmuring,
'Who was the woman in *Steppenwolf*?'
Left without saying goodbye
to my senior. Her last words:
'I need to tell you I dislike you.'

The Apology

Mosquitoes charged me with their sour sugar
outside the vinegar house. Six years, ten years,
sixty, it ferments from oak to juniper
to chestnut to cherry and back to oak wood barrels,
balsamic vinegar separating itself
from a hundred year old mother sediment.

Breathe in through the unstoppered hole.
Smell it changing. This is immortality
but that sweet vinegar didn't comfort my ill friend.
She hovered towards my slight sore throat.
I shouldn't have let her low immunity near me.
My virus would order us differently,

her life for one ciao, and down she goes
to that atomic level, eternal future,
for which our short lengthening time ferments us.
Next day I said to my body
(my body thinks my voice is God):
'You handle poison too well.

Your itch denies my taste for eternity,
it's anciently made.' Then my body said,
'I'm giving you time.' So I called to say sorry.

Separation

Snails might shout
crawling from mint to balm 'I burn'
or call from lovage and hosta

'I'm burning dry'
while my husband is falling asleep
in the sun away by Muker Beck,

where oyster catchers
freeze on their nests and only water stays
awake, irritably controlled, pushing

stones, stuck, stuck, stuck, stuck, till we both are
woken by pain with its orange beak.

Snail

Examine yourself, river.
Wind, you have collapsed
from your adrenalin rush.
Sun, you've flooded the vertical,
splashing reeds and palming
planes. Damaged oak,
you have no heart or gut.
Your only organ, skin.

I cling to you tighter
than a striped shell
on a fennel stalk.

TB Hospital, 1944

His nurse said: In the tar of the roof above
your ward, lichen patterns have the look
of Irish turfs after floods.

His chest inflated
like a pyramid, huge, with blank walls
built by hand and unexplained vents.

Folding the corners of his sheets to envelopes,
she described the Black and Tans, a haggard,
the taste of soda bread.

A translator can add only humility
to the original. She took away
his dish of spit. She found herself robbed

during their marriage, like a tomb. Doesn't death
grit the road with ice, she often said,
yet the sun hauls up each crystal?

Ad Astra

So strongwilled, the thumb of the sun
                                        on sea,
that its aquamarine flashes
like a poor contact. Eye-stinging flash, on off on.
Something dazzling has been wrong
                                        with me:

I've climbed through life looking up.
                                        These doors
grip the street's staircase as I do.
I'm shaded by further heights of terrace. Soft toys
lie on roof tiles below me –
                                        old lures.

The village has seen collapse
                                        in land-
slide and flood. Fishermen have drowned
in the bay, and poets. They're cold metal, these rails,
hardly warmed by the sweat of
                                        my hand.

Reaching the starry bushes,
                                        capers
springing from the ruined castle walls,
softening them like figs ripen on local thorns,
a rumpled packaging of
                                        lost wars,

having picked off some small fruits –

                                            I think

at last, 'Look down.' So does the sun:
electromagnetic solar waves are startling
sea waves to swink blank swink blank

                                      swink blank.

Cavalletta

Since she is labouring through summer seed –
one thousand feet above Castel Nuovo
I'm staring at the spot
as if ditch plants were the real vista,
horsetail, nettle, reed –
this grasshopper looks bulkier than rock

and this real mountain just an offcut mound.
I know nothing of grasshoppers. I see
her rocket-jumps, bits snapped
off compression. The bees and mayflies
float out of our bounds
while she clambers up a dandelion.

When I compare her to the flying boys,
only her big back leg has their stature
in sky. But they hold air
she can't capture. I feel I am slight
and shallow muscled.
Now I look upcrag, there is an angle

that renders grey mass foil, as tearable
as wings. Its own shale runs away. I spill
all thought of pinnacle.
She skates on the dirt around me, fired
by that proboscis.
Off. Up she spurts, deprivileging ground.

She levitates but then she lands upside down.
Down in the valley we use pediment
colour. We paint our doors
her shade of slate in rain like flakes torn
from rock. No back leg
can lift what I have floored to height again.

Alcyone

On an unfenced cliff, frightened
at the edge, in a million
silverfish of rain, I found

my sister Alcyone.
To me, it was just sand
crowning, a bitten earth

on which silt has built
for eight thousand years, an inch
a month. Still builds. She listened

to gulls whittle the neediness
of quiet. She watched a ship
slip into pearl while sunset

picked up importance. Look,
how brown bracken squats,
prickles with fragility

under squalls that dig into
the shoulder muscles of gusts. Gusts
that coil and bounce beyond all

elastic limit. Young winds.
Young winds I think like you.
I'm not over that hour,

Birthday

at last when I stepped out a wind
blew its throaty whistle behind
over me dead leaves butt-
ends the outlived mess of ribbon
road gutter flew
into my hair brightly coloured flies
I tried to keep my feet running
on the ball of ground
vacant blocked with broken crystal
a bit of mirror myself I crossed
the smallest lungs could have blown
me about as they wished hurled
into a brick niche presents
chewed off in my arms stuck
with scraps of *Best* and *Wishes*

Victorian Harvest, with Peacock

Then men wore yorks to keep mice down, subset
of universe evolved to view a world
not as physics would but, like me, flying
from field fire. So, courage...find a peacock,
bird at the top of its tail, tail five times
taller than bird, each eye of a feather
a foothold, ride that bent back neck, break in
to vertical, unrecognisable
fear. There world isn't just trouser for mice
even if sky is woven and land leg.

Jehanne d'Arc and the Angels of Battle

They were carrying elaborate armour, when they broke in,
to lock me in.

This metal face,
these sleeves can't be undone. I think I'll suffocate. This hard face

is so heavy that, in itself, it could kill. I pitied them
when I saw them;

since they flew off
I haven't always been believed in, myself. First they took off

great muscular structures from their shoulders. Those wings
        were steel.
Put me in steel,

I said. I was
not touched otherwise except to hear words ransack me. Word was,

soldiers pray to me as if I am what was brought of value.
What I value

inside metal
is, my galvanised skin thinks it's dominant. Helpless metal.

Against the Window

A small bird disturbs
the lulling leaves
whose unstable branches
seem to control it.

The Night of Misrule *a folktale*

You know that flabby sponge of thin-skinned land
where every soft heart has been swilled away?
Its Lord of Misrule
off on an irresistible job one night
mailed his caretaker to get in more drink.

But she dumped his car in a ditch and picked
a thick-skinned donkey to carry – not wine,
rum or gin. Her choice
was squash. The panniers sagged, the five hundred
kilo regional record pumpkin rode

pillion, sunk on its weight, bulging blue
veins netting its leather. Packed below pelt-
irregular crowds
of squashes, striped
green, yellow, orange,
nobbly,
cratered, warts
sawing smooth-skinned
balls and stools

alongside faux squash, The Hand of Buddha,
lemons poking claws at cuckoo melons.
These varieties
were rarely tasted in the Land of Misrule.
Buffalo moaned and spread their lips. Wild goats

jumped fences. Now the caretaker, Lady
of Misrule, cooked the obscure feast. How each
forgotten name wept
its oedematous inner life: Sweet Dumpling,
Small Sugar. Gnarled osseous forms

battered in their throes, hissed hard: 'It's heavy
hanging from stiff necks, texturing sun. We
mashed earth to hammocks
for our flesh.' Chartreuse, vanilla, beer brown hidden in the rigorous toughnesses groaned.

Midnight. A court was scratched to call for wine
but the donkey whinnied his evidence:
'She knows I suffer
from being stroked. He packs us so close in our pen
we make plates of each other. We're patient

while other teeth take the straws from our backs.'
An acid smell, chewed hay, pushed court muzzles
deep in the baked squash
till all was eaten. They were satisfied. Drink?
No one thought of it. The donkey hobbled

through offices braying out a new law:
No liquor here but tears of melted squash,
of Golden Acorn,
of Crown of Thorns, of Trumpet of Albenga.
Every essence in adamantine heard

and all soft-centred creatures petrified
and crystallised,
starched,
starkened,
corneous

dragged their callouses
and shattered
plashed,
quagged
churned the argillaceous land.
At dawn when the lord came home from work

he found a capital of sludge and mud.
His rage fermented into speechlessness.
The caretaker gripped
her donkey's carpeted flanks with sober heels
and hasn't been seen in Damp Valley since.

The Night Bacchus Let Us Down

So you're a No to our *Nonsense Night,* Bacchus?
What's wrong with our community? The ballroom pool
is one degree above perfection? But we've shared
an apple with the woman who leaves those free sheets
at the gates – she doesn't know the code
to open them, she's no guest – yet as surely
as she is nameless and her russet dust
hanging in our mouths isn't drinkable
so all our imperfections are invisible
to her. Yes, she has only a button to show
she's a god. Rain mark on silk this morning, now
she pulls sky down and we've crowned her low lights.
No dawn could ever be as bright as this
board of night she's chalked. We're flying,
ocean birds from bough to coral bough.
Watch our wings fin through this airy salt.

Orchardleigh

Constructive slaves, pennants in a line
frill constantly and on on on on on.
My favourite footpath over the fields disfigured
by bunting

from where sheep stand, frozen flags to church,
by the chapel itself, administered
by a photographer today. Once a lane led past,
not just to,

the chapel, a field's end, open once
a month on a Sunday. A Japanese
woman pauses when I ask who is wedding here: 'Nnn.'
Here's the bride,

subdued in an open car. Father
waves to the fields. Rolled wiring lies beneath
posts, thin gentle thornless wire. September wind, warm
as hair. Why

is this hidden wedding a surprise?
My marriage was made in a registry
office behind square hedges down an alley leading
over up-

thrust roots of planes to a secret lake
I never knew was there till later I
saw a blue eye on a map. The bridesmaids were children,
falling in

grass, upside down, star-shaped, brown speeding
oil. I acted so well, the audience
must have thought I was a passerby bride, artless, young,
can't project

her voice, winning by continual
smiles. Sacred is as hard to predict as
when a sunspot will flare from below the sun's surface.
Street and field

remain though office interiors
have gone. I see the children rush around
the register, push, sing. Out here they're forty.
The physics

of surface differs from what's inside,
so I can't penetrate things. I can't make
my body sacred. But 'the sky is borrowed'. Ageing
does not heal.

I've grown up piecemeal, collage, since that
gilt crown on a post, plentiful sand strewn
on concrete. My guests were spangled, strung out, torn. Question
it, The One,

The Wedding. I want this bride to. But
she needs to join, chooses bride-heavy join
-ery. Flesh is a cloud that weighed some tons last time it
was measured.

Pennants, you exhausted triangles,
coloured, cut, slight, ordered, hung, hoisted cloth,
tell her I'd celebrate if I were her friend. Crisscross
big windows,

give her a sense of sacred. Not so
tawdry, less responding like skirt. Striped air,
corral the guests again. They must flap and be frenzied
by wind, day

and night. Dance, she'll say. So, her will will
celebrate one person. They are pennant,
these two happened on. I'll sustain your materials
unpennant

wings to rope across my back on some
equinox of wedding, when day and night
are equal. For now, you can't know I'm alone. No lull
nor cheerstop.

The Witness

Other panickers had worn the marble steps
up to the first, on to the second storey,
towards caged aerial balconies.

The wooden rail to the top creaked at each run
of family. I could see myself falling
below the pine crown. Visitors leaked

out of the tower. I climbed down past the tidemark
of medieval sea, to an open square
where a black arm was being wrenched back

behind his own spine. I *can't breathe,* he cried, his
face pushed to the ground. *I'm going to witness this,*
I said. The policemen stood him, turned him,

to show he could breathe. His glasses were in place,
shattered. I've been back since. There are fossils there,
creatures that look like holes in the stone,

and a long view of evening light locks around
that muddied place as if the tower rides over
the sun till a corona blazes.

Graffitista

What do you make of this dangerous space,
the gutter? Children commandeer it and conjure
what they can from such silken dust as is
human and poor.

The street is full
of red, orange, yellow, green, all shapes, none
in good condition, exhausted from not drifting.
No one's guessed who it is who tags their walls.

Once my mother's name appeared on a piece
and Wikipedia says I am somebody
else, a mechanic. That would be my niece.
I paint shadow.

You can keep it
if you photograph it. Great galleries
pop from hands holding up cameras. I draw on.
One, many, male, female? Who is my sign?

Legend of Grey

After a smogbound pregnancy
her mother said her birth opened
a door locked in concrete.

Her colour was ashy plural,
cashmere black of storm, the silver
of heat. Suppose you've not

seen an eye ... her intense line of
grey around the iris, inside
colour's gazing circle,

glows from that flat unnamed mix of
wavelengths. Streets give way when she walks
but don't think they're water.

Not only black, not only white,
they're metal melting, brightness saved
heron-sharp from squalor.

Amber

A woman had missed a wake.
We'd just come from one.

I could still hear the chant
of Buddhists. A girl who'd gone

brought a message back –
there'd been a crash. Our coach

was stuck down there. We stamped.
The road took our reproach.

Meanwhile the crossing light
which was forbidding none

in red and none in green,
was challenged by a man

speaking a sort of Tennyson:
'Oh stay on amber, rest.'

The inaccurate machine,
like us, passed this test.

Heritage

'*Get That Tiger* isn't a hymn,' my mother
muttered under the muttering of the Mass.

Later, her Costa face tint showed up odd
against the plain Tudor Catholic walls.

The priests' hole behind a bookshelf was labelled
a library. 'Can't have had much learning,'

a blonde boy said. 'Douai,' said Father Thomas.
I scrambled down a ladder. At the bottom, soil.

'Not much they'd be doing here,' said Phyllis
'but praying.' It isn't a hymn. Monks were dressed

as celebrities. We photographed them laughing
by the moat. 'They dress up for visitors,'

Big Nurnie said. 'Cassocks.' My mother slapped
her sandwich down on her missal. My son kept on

about the ways they executed priests.
'Who is this *they?*' I asked. It isn't a hymn.

There comes a time when you switch off from listening
and lose someone. I traced her back to the hole.

O Mary, Mother of God, you get that tiger,
full of grace, and you sing her to us.

Concert

I forget my murderous husband
when an old friend visits. An old friend

I haven't seen for years. She's famous,
or her novels. I sing now, she says.

We listen in our largest room.
It's too small an auditorium.

We're audience, and the alliums,
those blue balloons of pins, a poster

of Angela Davis. It's hung here
since the day this old friend got married.

She sings six bars, her voice natural
as on her wedding day when she said

she hadn't washed, to be the more clean
for the commitment. What could be more

natural than that, listening to her,
I would forget my husband's anger?

He says he's never tried to kill me.
But he has. I was noisy with love.

The window was open to the street.
He pushed a pillow over my mouth.

Self Portrait as Windscreen

Do you think I'm clear on every issue
just because I'm glass?
Have you heard yourself calling 'Claire,

Claire, Claire, Claire' when you're confused?
A name is lulling
when you aren't clear on every issue.

So your favourite phrase 'Let's be clear
on this one thing'
is the public face of 'Claire. Claire.'

I see you everywhere, using my nature,
hardened from soft,
imagining you're clear. Fired, made

to soften, harden again. We're laminated.
The crack that comes
won't shatter us or your calling.

On Not Living Up to Early Promise

My soul is stuck with droplets of king
and impregnated with those bleach stains
of saint that you get before you're born.
I've rent this cloth life long. It's net now.
Pull it open like curtains, you'll see
a film of condensation. My skin
mimics the mist closing *Heaven's Gate*.

A Dormative for Strings

Say I'm suddenly called
to listen, to start from sleep when
my air is stroked by broad-rayed rain in bows
but I can see only the silent conductor,

a goddess bereft of
her creation, summoning
my existence to her high sound. I calm
to plantain, plain weed, strand on a resonance her

hand makes to hold my whole
halo of seeds. Her narrowed
eyes bring in my restlessnesses. She has
no instrument though she is one. She can't speak

and I can only see
a silent conductor. I
must tell you before we wake I've heard strings
shrinking to droplet dry in the oak of my bed.

Opponent

It was dark in the theatre.
I pulled the tube out of my throat
when the camera hit the empty spot
and rang against softness, trying
to take the measures I'd agreed.
The retch my stomach made was practical.
Pulling the tube out copied it.
The endoscopist's hands also
copied the retch. But I was the more shocked
to find I'd rushed towards those doors
with the large rubber flaps that shut
automatically behind trolleys
(like stomachs shut, not always well,
which is why I was there), and shocked
to hear the endoscopist calling me.
Not to swallow the tube again
nor hear how such procedures are
counter-intuitive but to be wrapped
in a white cellular blanket
on the bed. The two young nurses
who had held me too gently till I'd pushed
away, now wheeled me to the ward
past where the next patient waited.
I lay quiet and listened to the bark
of a wolf in a cave. I felt
its pelt sturdy enough to wreck
my oesophagus if I called to it.

It growled through my stomach's sphincter,
'I will spring. You won't be warned. No
idea you can hold to when I leap.'
My head is so small on my neck,
small camera that imagines
stomach as food bag. So stomach is, held
by me and another creature.
Not a wolf. Surely there is not
a wolf. Some other. I must be guarded.

Separation Season

Cold bamboo
was hatching, cross-hatching; dead
stem arches

aisled the field. Tractors decayed
at the edge.
Drivers had thrown to rot what

will not rot.
Our plan had wintered. Though
branches milled

their twigs to silver, still ice
crawled away
from what it had taken on

and the sun
stopped chasing mist to wire
and rays woke

mistletoe to emerald
on the oak.
Our jewels had nested here.

Diamonds,
opals begged *don't repeat us*
dissolve us.

Move, I said, now you can move.
Fissured field,
frozen for months, you've rested.

A Wanderer in End Erring Wood

The birch lives on outside its tree
in piles of logs, prepared to be useful.
Veneer, ply, plank. Walk
on it. Slam it shut. Bend
its new legs. Snappable saplings
are overleaved, a strength they'll lose.
Older birches' lower parts
are stripped of frailty. Look, they dance
in dark clubs. Hey ho, silver
shivering suns. Raw birch heart
gleams in the margins of my nails.
The trunks prevent paths by thickening
the forest, veiling grave-red houses,
if such sheer tines could
dispose of a grown blood filled woman,
if I get lost in End Erring,
find me. I'll be ankling over
stones. At least my backpack,
external organ full of function,
and my marks on snowy bark,
finally at ease with repetition,
find them, find them.

Infant Cemetery

No grown ups here
but me. Quarried
hill. Exposed chalk.
I'm sorry they're not old too,

that I complained
three times about
the thudding noise
a ball makes hitting a foot.

Death drops details.
There'll be no more
propped photographs,
a parrot topping Mai's pram,

Tariq cycling
across a round
biscuit into
the orange turn of sunset.

A parent should
be thorn, hook wind.
Wind never bleeds.
All who are committed to

this public space
of shade, play on
these grains of rock,
sand of our gigantic world.

Getting Carter

That men have no souls occurred
 to Mike Hodges, who begat
Carter who caught
a train north

for revenge
and found a girl
unsouled. That year, knitting, purl
one, plain one, I took a train,

ignored my waters breaking.
So I dropped a soul in to
the world too soon,
dropping like

vest, needles
on the track. Though
hidden variables show
why and how revengers kill,

you can't compare narrative
with human beings for value:
death's fun to view.
Look: Carter

is Hodges'
psychopathy
while my labour remade me
– maybe made more than remade.

Smoke

A single mother
has a baby and we
either ignore the colour or we think

it's the prettiest
of all colours, or point
to cigarettes or offer knitted things

and read her future
as easily as leaf
through an anthology of Greek riddles

like the one that asks
who is the different-
skinned child of a mother. Answer: the one

who's a wingless bird
clever enough to fly
into such clouds as she herself who makes

eyes tidal with tears
as soon as minds take in
how she dissolves in air when she is born.

Lullaby

Time to sleep. The torsos,
the armless, the footless,
the headless are locked away.

Sleep, sleep. We will not stop
real bodies waking
to their ends while galleries

re-issue flesh differently.
Sleep. Bronze parts exhale
ghosts that take steps beyond

plinths. Go to sleep, leave
fragments to fashion, dead
sculptors to pace above

artless, sleepless.

On Narrowness

because we stand
between stacks like
librarians
walls form small space
vertical hard
to move in but
caryatids
everywhere
welcome our love

Requisition at Abinger

By ponds damming the Tillingbourne
he strikes a bell with his hammer.

By ponds damming the Tillingbourne
hammer men made chains and hooks
on this common land, disparked
to give wood for the mills. My love

(whose need I am going to supply)
is in the first stages of sainthood –
God is giving him things… I'm such
a thing, a bunch of watercress,

more stalk than leaf. The painted smith
opens the clock to sound me out.

He strikes a bell with his hammer.

The Scour

On a trawl at the moment, River Mole.
I know, mad. This screw of leather slime
is an old shoe. The mud's as smooth as skin.
Thank you very much! Are you coming
to live with me then? It's a crispbag day.

Snappy. The freezer box weighs a ton
strapped across my shoulders. Plastic apron
lets wet in like a broken dam. Good of you.
Looking forward to it when you're free.
Stopping a mo. Rinsing my boots with one hand.

Actually that's the sound of naked feet.
Victorian tide waitresses grazed the Thames,
like me, for trash, worth even less then
and they were barefoot. I found something, love
letters in a metal box, readable.

Just. A man who lived on the bank maybe.
His affair. Yes, well yes. D'you reckon his wife
threw them in the river? And he saw her do it
so, when the flood rose, he'd come out and watch
for the water to stop this thresh and turn back

to a quiet lap? Useless. I'm off to the Tillingbourne.
Find the lost seal of King John. When, then?
Bring how much stuff? Some kids are calling,
Listen. I'm holding the phone towards the bridge:
What are you waiting for, they're shouting, *a boyfriend*

on the Titanic? I can see him clearly
leaning against one of those garden gates
meant to lock the river out, his girlfriend
searching the other bank for pennyroyal,
women's herbs like rue and hellebore.

Snow at Christmas

I've thought of snow as a raptor that seizes
holly,
ivy, all the evergreens, a dog that bites
a child
near the eye. It turns to dirt. I'm used to trees
that rear
and don't lean towards me or bow down like this.
I stopped
to sense temporal and carotid points of
welcome
and the snow ushered me into the garden's
charge, pink
sky packaged as a giant jay's breast, puffy
and shy
on a witch hazel. We haven't read a word
since then
all Christmas but proper names, prepositions
and love.

None in the Pot

Fondue, dated as it is, hinted at you:
collapsed, cooling heart but now I see flash had been caught.

Fondue, dated as it is, hinted at you:
the set-aside, sitting, cutting bread in pieces
small enough to lose in sticky cheese, making forfeits –
I insisted that you stand on one leg singing
'Keep Right on to the End.' Stirring held our orbit
from wandering sociability. I suspect you'd seen me
push sun upsky to find you. So after we had mopped
the molten Emmental, what made such dry tack in that furnace?
I said, nun in the pot, la religieuse; you called it le reste
or a pulsar, remnant of a sun's explosion, stellar body all thrown off,
collapsed, cooling heart but now I see flash had been caught.

UFood

for Geraldine Monk

You're amsweet, you're agribitte, you're ayl.
You're boshmop, you're blannues, you're boolish.
You're case-popped, you're culpeta.
You're dashup.
Eggsound, eece, eantie.
Femashee, frain, you're all too farx.
You're goeshlivmicurmic.
You're hoth, hith, huth, hith again.
You're inmithed.And you're always jecly or at least jey.
You're krattles at the weekend. Kerp.
You're lacemad fillets of freshwater.
You're every munkid I ever cooked.
You're nurma, you're nedbaked, you're nipwhisked.
You're always ooove. Admit it, you're oan.
You're not pixtunt yet (that's bitter).
Yet you're quolle.
You're radfedling, you're rochgon.
Every cafe wants to get your shurth.
You're toomix, thegm, terpinaded.
U are food U are.
Vismette, vash, vret-vret.
Wilobess, rare wussage.
You're xaited, you've been xaix to me.
You're Y I eat yoos-yoos.
For ever zlip.

Vial as I Am

Am I not
a casket for bones?

Am I not
a keen enough lover to want a vial
of his lost fat, cloudy or clear,
to be worn like a locket
of fading hair?

To tie in a ribbon his Body Mass Index
(though this measures fat indistinguishably
from bone and muscle, ligament, blood)?

Yet isn't the living underskin,
itself a carpenter of flux,
a casket for bones?

The Candidate Goes Home

Is it there it is relief relief more red.
Cars stolen than any other shade buggered.
If I'll change colour for idiots minutes.
Into the boot my contacts book oh jesus.
Tuesday what time OK OK OK OK lots.
Of time all this carry in out every sod.
That Elder cat another dove she gets dove-.
Cote he gets car old joke I get power has.
To be me they're definitely going to.
Do it call one lose let me in why don't cats.
Eat the sodding lock the back door oh oh oh.
Get fresh parsley my health experiment men.
And health they get the worst and do they care could.
Those two facts be connected doc July rain.
Best kind he is as good as any orange.
Blossom don't chain it he's got to get in hell.
More white feathers starving silk thing very short.
Too good not the yellow bra the blue skinny.
Off with thirteen nights out bit of cream what is.
That strangulated flesh I never starving wine.

Gold Moment, 3000 AD

We chose to be made immortal in our garden at sixty degrees.
Our bench was commissioned from Big Elite Metal.
They pop by to shine the alloy, almost as often as we're serviced.
Our thoughts on never dying have been etched to flash
            permanently on
the kitchen window. Those herbs can't help now but oh
the smell of bergamot. Keith never dozes. He's reading two pages
of *The Burning Answer*. I try to think a poem through glaze. It fails.
Revisions involve change in time. We ordered this:
Gold Moment. Don't imagine we're not alive in it. Our hearts beat,
our blood pours through, we are warm. The children hate it.

Who Was I?

If I had care of my young self now, I'd say stop it,
don't meet him again
and let love withdraw.
But then
energy

was potential. Our serendipitous encounters
have come to some good
yet I'd warn her
amply
to get out.

I can't now say heave your worries over to future
knowledge. I can't hear
who I was, under
purple
stemmed green beans.

That scratch of stalk stood fur-eared after fruit. When will I
catch myself up, when
will I go back, stroll
our field?
Can't do it.

Power's the point energy acts at. So much for lost
oxygen, so much
for heat released by
breaking
bonds. I'm done.

But Anaximander envisaged sun as a hole
showing fire outside.
and I have lived to
weather
poor physics.

Infatible

I've always thought
over is almost all of lover.

I've always thought
I was infatible
in my sealed-in stuff that oozes energy.
I've avoided naming a bomb
Fat Man.
I've considered variants such as
Lo, Low, Lite, Lyte, concluding
they are the signs of an idiotocracy.
And I still think the word 'overfat'
must be a value judgment since I know
over is almost all of lover.

Rockborne

Our friends are scrambling towards the top stone stretched
like wall. I hope they sit on it and wave.
The wind has mounted those yew trees.
They're not upright nor our friends.

Left here, we doze watching the oystercatchers
who sit like us. Eggs may be beneath them.
It's June but no bird will be born
from those cold eggs left in rocks.

Look, lichen, you prefer not to broadcast spread.
But by wind, paw or palm rubbing pollen-
coloured curls, you'll send new climbers
next year. So, friends! Stop now, wave.